SHILP-Kaavya

Love, Opportunity & Random Thoughts

ShilChat

SHILP-Kaavya

First published in 2020 by

Becomeshakespeare.com

One Point Six Technologies Pvt Ltd,

119-123, 1st floor, Building No. J2,
Wadala East, Wadala Truck Terminal,
Mumbai, Maharashtra 400037, India
T: +91 8080226699

ISBN
ISBN - 978-93-90266-14-2

About the Author

Hey! My name is Shilpi Chatterjee
(Pen Name: ShilChat).

I always enjoyed reading,
writing and traveling.

As a writer anything and
everything inspires me.

'Go with the flow /process' is how I am in
writing and in life. Believe that everything is
in abundance, we need to look at it
and accept the best. And the best will
happen to you. Let it happen!

*"A word- A line - A question - A paragraph -
A character - A short story -
A painting - A quote -
A book - Anything can inspire - to fully
express that will inspire another."*

Preface

About the book

This book is about - Love, Opportunity and Random Thoughts

Foreword

In my book, I relate the changes brought about in my life with my experiences. You'll find interesting poems and mementos that I hope will touch your heart.

Dedication

I ask the indulgence of my son who may read this book for dedicating it to grown-ups. I have a serious reason: he is the best friend I have in this world. I have another reason: he understands everything, even books about children. To my parents, my sister, relatives and all my friends who deserve the great relationships we have .

For a close samaritan, who made me put the dragons in.

Thanks to..

Also a special thanks to all the very amazing poets and writers who were an inspiration to publish this work.

SHILP KAAVYA
{Love, Opportunity and Random Thoughts}.

SHILP-Kaavya
(Love-Opportunity-Random Thoughts)

LOVE (29 VERSES)

OPPORTUNITY (37 VERSES)

RANDOM THOUGHTS (35 VERSES)

SHILP-Kaavya

 LOVE

MOM

Her Love Is As Rustic
As An Old Decor
That Reflects A Rustic Sensibility
Made In A Plain and Simple Fashion.

Sometimes I talk to my son about life,
Often he surprises me with his words,
Have always noticed him grow every day.
A nest full of love, compassion and
benevolence,
Mighty he rise and shine for all.

Sometimes my heart leaps and bounds,

Under the wings of love,

So you are the one with who -

Heart and soul showed me -

A new beginning of today.

Not giving up for a second,

Time and again sowing the seed of love.

What Is Love?

It is an experience of many feelings -

Happy, Excitement, Romantic, Cheated,

Hated, Ignored, Slashed And

It is an experience of many thoughts -

Beauty, Sexy, Lovable, Huggable, Disgusting,

Irritating, Loud and

It is these experiences that determines

What Is Love?

There Is Experiences and There Is Love..

So Darling... Do You See..

Love Is Love

Love Love

Be Love

Live Love.

Family

Convincing my family is like...

Adams Family

A delight in the comfort and

unaware of the bizarre

Yet appealing and delightful.

The Other Child

Yes! I am the other child,

Who can see you, feel you and understand you.

No matter how much I want to -

I can't respond to you.

Don't think I do not have feelings or thoughts or a mind,

Yes! I am the other child,

Who eagerly waits to be hugged, kissed and taken abreast.

And the eyes keep hunting for an approval of acceptance.

Yes! I am the other child,

Whose thoughts don't matter,

Whose tears just roll down waiting to be heard just once and with lots of effort I said it - "Maa"

Respect Me.....

Respect Me For I Am A Mother

Respect Me For I Am A Daughter

Respect Me For I Am A Sister

Respect Me For I Am A Wife

Respect Me For Who I Am

Respect Me For What I See

Respect Me For What I Feel

Respect Me For What I Do

Respect Me For What I Love

Respect Me For Being Me

Respect Me For Where I Go

Respect Me For How I Do

Respect Me For Why I Do

Respect Me So That I Can Respect You!

LOOP-ed

*He sat with his arms looped around his knees,
near the road that loops around the pond.*

*At the far end of the loop, she waited for him,
to be held tight and his arms looped around
her for all the comfort she is looking for.*

*Alas! She waits near the end of the road that
loops around the pond.*

When will they wake up and unwind the loop?

Isn't it time they mend it, tear it down.

*How long will they keep sitting at the end of
the loop waiting?*

*Waiting for the loop to unbend and unwind
as the strings of heart that's attached cannot
be broken.*

Let the loop unbend and unwind.

Let it!

Being Happy Is Everything because it allows one to build oneself

And defines a character in itself.

Smile of a child

Smile of a child is like a golden chariot that shines so bright

Smile of a child is like the colours of the rainbow that radiates bright light

Smile of a child is like a beautiful coral that is shiny and white

Smile of a child is the ray of sunshine that brings hope all around

Smile Oh Child Smile with care

Don't let anyone take it away from you

Smile is the prized possession no matter what can never be taken away

Smile of a child gives a reason, a reason to laugh, love and get lost to get lost in the coming future

A future so bright just like a Smile Of A Child.

It's not about

The love you get from others that makes you feel loved.

It's about

The love you give yourself that makes you feel loved and fulfilled.

They asked me what's my religion?

I said, "None, I don't want to live with any condition to accept and love people or animals around."

Born Different..

We All Are Born Different

With Different Colours of

Skin, Hair, Eyes.... Or

With Different types of

Limbs, Face, Body.... Or

With A Difference

Blind, Dumb, Deaf...

We All Are Born Different

What we don't have different is

A Heart to Love, Respect, Embrace

Let's Respect the Heart that each has

Let's Give Kindness, Trust, Greatfulness

We All Are Born Different and

Humanity Binds Us Together.

Celebrate

Life Is A Celebration

Mark It As A Happy Event

An Affair, An Occasion to Jubilation.

I can live with the..

The lovely memories of Us

Even when you are not around

I Love You So...

If You Paid For Every Word You Spoke

I would have chosen words of compassion and benevolence

So that my Pandora's box is filled with treasure of aliveness, acceptance and embracement.

Consider: Love is a word.

What we experience when in love

Determines our belief in love.

It is in action and experience that

Makes us who we are in love.

Doormat

What do you think I am?
A Doormat,
Pushing, Pulling, Giving, Taking
Leaving me all bruised.
What do you think I am?
A Wuss,
Humiliating, Abusing, Mistreating, Ridiculing
Leaving me all crushed.
Will I not be loved?
Will I not be listened?
Will I not be cared for?
Am I asking too much or
Is it that I am
Not Welcome!
Give me a sign of hope.
Give me a sign of faith.
Give me a sign that will -
Help me live -
Before it's too late.

LOVE

Feelings come and go

It's not permanent

Don't run behind it

To hold it.....

It will go away and

You will stand all

Confused and Muffled.

Our Love IS the Universe

Where one can find Solitude

And Travel Is like The Diary of

Events which keeps Growing and

Last probably Eternity.

COULD THIS BE THE SECRET TO SUCCESS?

*The cold wires of my body can feel
connected to yours with an intensity and
the commitment towards each other which
is never felt or seen before.*

*The cold wires of my body can feel connected
to yours –
to touch , feel and melt in each others arms.*

*The cold wires of my body can feel
connected to yours. Just Connected.*

Be Connected.

LOVE

I believe that...

When we see nature's beauty is a symbol of angel around you

When we see animals saving humans or humans caring for animals is a symbol of humanity

When we see poors been fed and children been educated is a symbol of compassion and love

When one fights for another or group is a symbol of freedom

Fighters who win peace noble prize is a symbol of peace for the nation.

You Know It's Love When...

Insecurities Fade Away.

Challenges Come With A Smile...

The Experience Is Lively & Fulfilled.

Tum aa gaye ho

Ab zindegi ka safar lagey pyaara sa

uss bacchi ki muskaan jaisi jo

maa ki godh may khelne ke liye na jaane

kitne barson se ruki huyi thi.

Our Coffee Cups Speak of Love, Deep
Thoughts and Sex.

Shaam hone ko hain,

Baarish aisi baras rehi hain,

Maano jaisi bahut pyaasi hain,

Uski nazar jaise kisi ke intezaar may hain.

Roz shaam aati hain magar -

Aaj ki shaam kucch khaas hain,

Meri nazar tumhare intezaar may hain,

Kaha ho tum ke yeh dil bekaraar sa hain.

Shaam hone ko hain,

Aa-jaon ab toh tum aa-jaaon,

Meri nazar tumhare intezaar may hain,

Shaam hone ko hain.

Jab Tum...

Jab Tum Nehi Thay

Tum Yaad Aaye, Bahut Yaad Aaye,

Vo Haseen Shaamein Aur

Vo Pyaari Raatein.

Jab Tum Nehi The

Tum Yaad Aaye, Bahut Yaad Aaye,

Vo Tumhara Kabhi Ruthna Aur

Vo Tumhara Kabhi Hasna.

Jab Tum Nehi The

Tum Yaad Aaye, Bahut Yaad Aaye,

Vo Beetey Din Unn Galiyon May Aur

Vo Beetey Raat Humare Aangan May.

Adhuri Kahaani..

Jab koi Safar hum shuru karte hai

Ek adhuri kahaani

Ek adhura silsila

Shuru Ho jaati hai

Jeevan Rekha Kitni Choti

Jitni Ek Maa Ka Pyaar Apne

Bacche Ke Liye...

Asha Uss Toonti Huyi Rekha Se Judi

Jo Banate Banate Ruk Gayi

Phir Uth Khadi Huyi

Jeevan Rekha Ko Banate Huyi...

Haar Na Maanenge Buss

Jeevan Rekha Banate Chale Jaayenge

Jeevan Rekha Kitni Choti

Jitni Ek Maa Ka Pyaar Apne

Bacche Ke Liye

Sheher ke sabhi raste gaaon tak nehi aate...

Rishte jo banaye the vo kaha gaye?

Har uss pugh-dandi par meri nigah hai...

Jo raaste gaaon aur sheher ko ek karta hai

Issi soncch may ke dono raaste ek
ho jaaye aur

kabhi sheher ke sabhi raaste gaaon
tak bhi aaye.

SHILP-Kaavya

OPPORTUNITY

An Opportunity Is What All One Needs- the race, religion, colour, disability, differently able All.... Everyone comes together and excels till each and everyone starts to show-case their talent.

Nothing else is left to show or compare to other than growth.

Life is about getting and giving opportunities to excel, to soar high, to break free from the old beliefs and thoughts.

Just embrace love, joy and oneness.

Creativity has no boundaries

It only has ideas and thoughts and feelings and action

Brown Wooden Bar

Standing behind the brown wooden bar,
Seperating me from the people in the room.
Giving me time to think of my past -
"What did I do? Was it wrong? "
I had to feed my family that's all.
When I was young - I didn't educate
myself and was busy toiling around in the
neighbourhood with few friends.
Snatching whatever came my way,
Believing it would bring me power and
strength.
Oh! How I wish, I listened to my heart and
not my mind for the cheap thrills.
See where I am standing today -
Behind the brown wooden bar.
The judgement will be given to me where I
will be behind the steel bar for harming the
innocent people throughout my life.
Only if I could turn back time.
If I could only!

The problem is there is no problem

*There is only opportunities to soar high
and wide.*

OPPORTUNITY

Tales Of Hopes Came

From His-Story

The History That Allowed Us

To Create A Future For The

Generations To Come.

Hoping For The Best And

Waiting For The Change In

In The Midst Of All The Chaos.

2 Minute Recipe for a Happy life

Make a cup of tea and sit by the window,
enjoying the morning fresh air that carries a
flight of believes that the day will be
Great and Smile!

OPPORTUNITY

Paper planes gives us hope to fly.

It expresses freedom, joy, love and courage.

*For its light weight takes courage to soar
high and soar low,*

*to feel the wind slipping below it,
to feel the - freedom, joy and love.*

*In life too keep your feet on the ground, and
let your heart soar as high as it will.*

*With courage let it feel the freedom,
joy and love.*

*Am deciding my future and
Each are deciding their future and have the
power to make their present beautiful.*

*If only they could focus inwardly and not
outwardly for everything lies within them.*

*Have the courage to give up others dream
and build their own.*

*Don't be caught up with what others have
done or doing or will do,*

*Look upon one-self and tell one-self what
have you done or what will you do or what
will you be doing.*

Dear Night Owl

*The early bird starts to retreat for the night
and you my friend stay up past midnight.*

*You must be brighter and probably creative
like a writer who writes at night.*

Often have your best ideas at midnight.

*It's almost like staying up those extra
hours - unlocking a portion of your mind.*

So! How active are you through-out the day?

If I could make a Film..

*There would be shades of colours which the
naked eyes couldn't see.*

*Stories of stray dogs whose love were not
seen and
it's innocense were crushed like it never
mattered.*

*There would be lots of smiling children
and aged hands whose compassions were
to be felt.*

Roll - Camera - Action.

OPPORTUNITY

Outside my window I see...

A group of boys playing cricket

And an occasion shout of "How's That?"

The rain pouring heavy and dogs sliding
under the car to keep themselves dry,

Mothers with umbrellas and children -
jumping in the poodle of water,

A bird on the tin roof like a spectator -
watching everything at its purview.

An old man walking, birds flying and cars
zooming by.

Neighbours chit-chatting, leaves swaying
sheepishly like they are

Acknowledging everything around.

Pay Attention To ---

Building A Soulful Community.

Honouring Each Relationship ---

Making Your Intention Known.

Plan A Time ---

Hobbies, Personal Interests, Career.

Taking An Action ---

Sharing Your Intention Honestly.

Tool Box

There is a Tool Box to Mend Everything

An hammer to nail the wall

A screwdriver for nails

A stethoscope for patients

A measuring tape to measure

Tools are many bender, clincher, comb, fork,

garden tool, grappled, plough

And more stored in the Tool Box.

We Miss Out! The Tool Box of Life..

Family, Nature, Care-givers, Care-takers,

Happiness, Forgiveness, Compassion, Love,

Oneness, Friendship ...And More

Stored in Abundance...

...When we embrace the stored

Tool Box of Life

*I turn my back to love, smile, hugs,
music, imagination, reading, writing,
tea when I believe something better is
coming my way.*

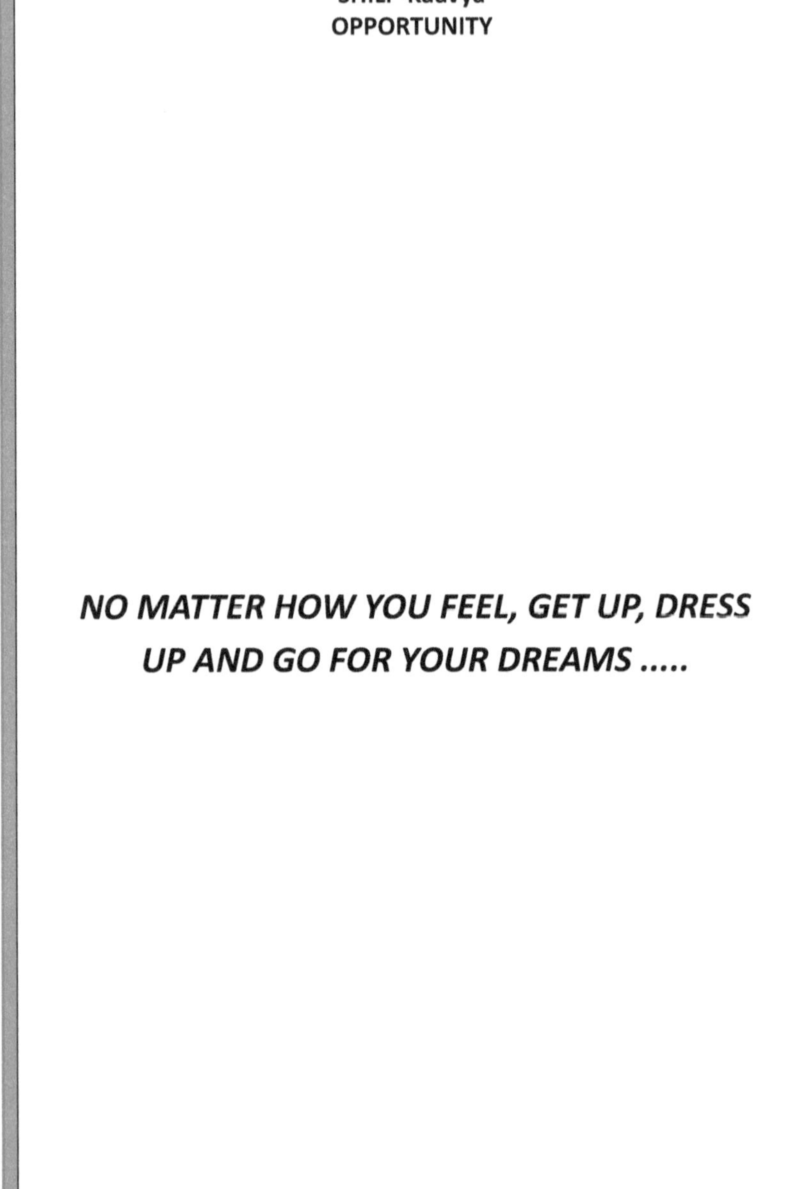

NO MATTER HOW YOU FEEL, GET UP, DRESS
UP AND GO FOR YOUR DREAMS .....

[45]

It is these brushes that I can paint with

Make my life the way I want it

*Use the bright colours, mix them with love,
joy, happiness and keep mixing till it spreads
to everyone and everywhere.*

BELIEVE

The Glass Is Both Half Full & Half Empty

#If You Believe It To Be True.. It Is True.

#If You Believe It Isn't True... It Is Not True.

How To Fight With Death?

Like Birth, Death is inevitable.

In-between of Birth and Death

Be a warrior

Be a brave heart

Be a saviour

Be a hero

Be a goal seeker

Be Compassionate,Futuristic,Loving such
that you are remembered to

Have Fought Death.

LAUGHTER THERAPY

Courage To Laugh At Yourself

Rather Than Others

You....Be..

It's The Strength That Causes

Confusion and Fear

You Are Unique.... Be Bold

Take Off The Mask

And Be You...

What is Stopping You from Exploring?

Is it the society or your neighbours or your family or your own thoughts

When The Mask Is Off ...

See What Is Available For You And

How Much You Can Do...

Take Off The Mask

And Be You...

-

OPPORTUNITY

We blame the Government

For things not done

Which We Should Have Done Long Back

When The World Was Created

All Was In Abundance and Free For
All Species.

Humans Put A Price Tag To It

With Limited Resources for Limited Species.

Sympathy

"Hey! Let me give you some food, cloth and money since you cannot afford it, I feel bad for you". He said to the beggar.

Empathy

"Hey! Would you like to wash my car and bike every day? You can earn - buy some food and cloth for yourself. You will not need to beg again". He said to the beggar.

The walls of my body

May seem fragile But

I Am Strong From With-In And

The Unsung Hero Of My Life.

Stories Are A Creation

Create It To Your Benefit

Make It Happy & Loving

Need: Few : To Live : Satisfactory :
Abundance

Water, Air, Shelter, Food ....

Want: Never Ending: Survival: Expectation

Family, Love, Marriage, Money, Car, House,
Children, Career and many more ...

To Make A Change Is Temporary

We Need To Transform Like...

Like A Caterpillar To Butterfly

And The World Need Not Look Back.

SHILP-Kaavya
OPPORTUNITY

When feeling lost

I find meaning in

Hugging my dog, Laughing With My Son,
Driving Around The City With My Love,

Dancing to my favourite music Or
Writing & Reading.

If Only Love Was As Strong As Hate

There Would Be No Boundaries

More Greeneries, More Traveling and
There Would Be Loving Relationships

And Much More....

I survive the day

To create magic

To create abundance

To create to an extent that

It's not survival anymore.

It's Creation. That gives me Power.

Life is about making right things and going on..

Until you realise that there is no right and wrong.

It has always been about the choices, and if those choices took you towards exploration or tardiness.

Inquire. Go on....

Crisis is an unstable Situation

That can be an Opportunity

Towards Creating New and Different.

You Are Bigger Than Who You Think

You Are...

Cause It.

*Two Perfect People Think They Are Imperfect
For Each Other*

- Irony!

*Looking For Perfection When Imperfection Is
What Makes Them Perfect*

- Dramatic Irony!

Duniya rang birangi college ki

Kabhi campus may ghoomna aur kabhi canteen may masti karna

Kabhi yeh stall toh kabhi vo stall

Kabhi teacher ki daant khaana aur vohi teacher ki pyaar bhari shabd sunna

Kabhi aankhon ke kone se crush ko dekhna aur kabhi paper par likh kar doston ki ore phekna

Kabhi college chodne ki gum may doob jaana aur kabhi re-union ke intezaar may behud khush hona
Aisi hai duniya rang birangi college ki.

Teetliya khwaab dekhti hain

Kab Vo apne kamla se bahaar aayengay

Iss rang beerangi duniya ki sayer karenge

Aur Jo Khwaab Sajaaye The Unhe
Poora Karenge.

SHILP-Kaavya

RANDOM THOUGHTS

My Right To Privacy Starts With
8 to 10 Characters
Which Includes Upper-Case, Lower Case,
Special Characters and Numbers.

And All The glory of Humanity Ends In The
Midst of Setting Up Privacy Settings.

One should never struggle against the INEVITABLE.

Insensibly one begins to twist facts to suit theories, instead of theories to suit facts.

*Every part of our body and every function of
our body is perfect and normal,
natural and beautiful.*

It's not about

The beast inside of you.

It's about

The beauty that lies with-in you.

One Cannot Hammer Their

Own Boat

In The Middle Of An Ocean Just Because

They Are Frustrated

Have You ever seen an Alien?

It is Unknown to Me.

For If You ever See a Floating Ship,

Say 'Hurray' and Call an Agency for

You will be 'Famous' I say.

Everyone is a FOOL....
A Shakespearean Fool and
A Medieval Fool.

The Shakespearean Fool -
the clever ones that use their wits and
The Medieval Fool - an entertainer
to entertain him and his people around.

Each Fool looks at the other and says:
"What a FOOL!"

S-E-L-F-I-E

Smile Please

Excited

Leave everything aside

Family & Friends Included

Increase FB and Instagram Posts

Eager to share it with all

What is KARMA?

Keep a positive attitude

Action to speak louder than voice

Respect every human and animal

Master the art of living and loving

Always be grateful and thankful.

We Live... We Dream.. We Conquer

*When GOD Has Created Different Colours
to Appreciate*

WHY

*Differentiate Them and Show the Selfishness
of the Human Mind!*

Grandfather: Muffin's saline is over

Grandson: Yes yay

Grandfather: He is better now

*Grandson: "Yay!!!!!"Muffin would have
said if he could talk*

If the walls could speak...

What would they say?

What it heard, what it saw and what it felt.

E-x-p-e-c-t-a-t-i-o-n

Sitting In A Room For Months

To Create Reality Out of Expectation.

R-e-a-l-i-t-y

Get Out There and Create The Expectation
To Reality.

Do you see those innocent eyes of the child
standing at the corner

Looking towards the life

Which is filled with treasure of aliveness,
love, hope, joy and fulfillment.

As time passed by, they faded away for the
innocence was lost, criticised, judged

And made wrong.

When will it STOP?

We should rejoice and relive the child
standing at the corner with the same
aliveness

And enthusiasm that it had.

I don't speak everything I think because that
gives away the power to someone
else which

I don't agree to.

These City Lights Are Too Dark

Which Reflects In Our Heart.

"He said...She said"

He said, "It's very messy again."

*She said, "That's Good. After the mess,
It will look beautiful."*

Traveling In Train is like a wedding house

There are all kinds of people, talks and a subtle madness

I know women....

Who has given up being a daughter

I know women....

Who has given up being a mother

I know women....

Who has given up being a sister

I know women....

Who has given up being a wife

I know women....

Who has given up being a sportswomen

I know women....

Who has given up smiling

I know women....

Who has given up life

Don't Give Up...

There is lots in store for you.

I just saw relationships blooming, smiling, hugging, exciting...

Places like restaurants, festivities and occasions.

It's like "limited edition" and they come with "conditions applied" too.

Everyone needs a 2AM friend to have coffee

or go for a long drive or just talk on phone...

So both days and nights are taken care off.

They Saw Him and They Gave Up On Him.

She said, "I Never Gave Up On You, My Child and Yet You Had To Go Away."

"It's Enough!" They Say To Each Other.

What is?

"All The Unrest and Noise Within".

Just Let Go.

*Look around and consider Yellow is just one
of the many colours like
Blue, Green, Black, Yellow, Red and Orange*

*Tomorrow you may find happiness in
another colour like Red 'Colour of Romance,
Love and Valentine's Day'*

*Like Happiness colour Yellow is not
permanent -
Use the water colour and that washes away
or a flower and that withers away*

Happiness is in Accepting.

*Yes I Accept Colour Yellow has its Own
Essence and Vibrancy.*

Let's Celebrate 'Sunshine'.

Thinking Out Loud

*To break this chain of hatred, envy, jealousy,
doubts, fear, rampaging souls*

And engaging in the lifting up of souls.

There is a thin line between -

'Fight and Flight'

Fight with your inner self and flight away from insecurities, doubts and fears.

Both gives a chance to destroy and make oneself.

Destroy Oneself or Make Oneself.

Go On... Be Brave.

Weird

Weird as Weird it may sound

The Weirdo has the Weirdest way of

Turning round which makes it Weirder than Weirdest.

So Weird is as mysterious as the Weirdo next door who I think is an alien.

And that is Weirder than the Weird who is reading this Weird poem.

All you saw was my exhaustion and bags
under my eyes.

What about my hard work and perseverance
I gave so many years?

To grow with compassion, love and support
for you.

Couldn't you see that?

*I used to say what people wanted to hear
but now I speak what I want to say.*

Let's Escape

Breakaway from the madness that's going on in the mind

Jump... Run... FFffrrreeee...

And again... Every second.

Mera mann yayawar ho chala hai,

Jaise ek banjaran...

Kabhi iss gali toh kabhi uss gaaon.

Chaahe apne aap ko main laakh rok loon
lekin yeh mann ko kaun rokey?

Samay Hain Mere Pass

Yeh Bhi Toh Ek Accha Bahanaa Hai

Khali kamra....

Jhoom Jhoom ke naachu aur gaaoon

Ke aayi dekho milan ki bela...

Kitna zaruri hai

Jaane wale kay saath bhi

Rishtey ka hona

Sonccho toh Jitna zaroori...

Ek patang ka udna

Asal may kucch bhi nehi

In conclusion.....

....."Yes, I thought, laying down my pen in extreme fatigue, I have had my vision."

Till my next..

Thank you

Shilpi Chatterjee..